Beningfield's Woodlands

Beningfield's Woodlands

GORDON BENINGFIELD

VIKING

VIKING

Published by the Penguin Group
Penguin Books Ltd, 27 Wrights Lane, London W8 5TZ, England
Penguin Books USA Inc., 375 Hudson Street, New York, New York 10014, USA
Penguin Books Australia Ltd, Ringwood, Victoria, Australia
Penguin Books Canada Ltd, 10 Alcorn Avenue, Toronto, Ontario, Canada M4V 3B2
Penguin Books (NZ) Ltd, 182–190 Wairau Road, Auckland 10, New Zealand
Penguin Books Ltd, Registered Offices: Harmondsworth, Middlesex, England

First published by Viking 1993
1 3 5 7 9 10 8 6 4 2
First edition

Foreword by Ian Cameron
Edited and designed by Ian Cameron
Produced by Cameron Books, PO Box 1, Moffat, Dumfriesshire DG10 9SU, Scotland

Filmset in Baskerville by Cameron Books, Moffat
Colour reproduction by Brian Gregory Associates, St Albans
Monochrome reproduction by Amber Graphics, London
Printed in Italy by Artegrafica, Verona

A CIP catalogue record for this book is available from the British Library

ISBN 0–670–840017

Among the books that have been consulted during the compilation of the text,
Cameron Books is particularly indebted for factual information to Oliver
Rackham's *Trees and Woodland in the British Landscape* (Dent, 1990 edition) and
Peter Marren's *Woodland Heritage* (David & Charles, 1990)

I would like to extend my thanks to Dr Peter Harper
and Professor Dr Willy De Loecker.
G.B.

PICTURES

Woodlands

If you follow an inviting path or track into the depths of an old wood, you will find yourself surrounded by evidence of traditions that go back hundreds, even thousands of years. It could be that none of the trees themselves are particularly ancient, but the wood as a whole may well have developed continuously in ways shaped by humans since time immemorial. Along the way, it will have acquired a rich population of animals and plants, and this, too, will have been influenced, though not necessarily on purpose, by human activities.

Although woods can seem wilder and more natural than anywhere else, particularly in the agricultural countryside that covers most of England, there is probably no woodland that is in anything like a primeval, undisturbed state, nor has there been for perhaps a thousand years. The seemingly natural beauty of our woodlands is something that we owe to the activities of our ancestors – and owe to our descendants to preserve for them.

The Britain left behind by the retreat of the glaciers at the end of the most recent Ice Age, some thirteen thousand years ago, was covered in bleak tundra and moorland, which the first trees colonised from the south as the climate became warmer. In the vanguard came the arctic sallows, aspens and birches. These were replaced first by pines, then by oak and alder, which were joined by lime and elm and later by ash, beech, maple, hornbeam and holly.

In 4500 BC, almost all of Britain was covered in what the countryside historian Oliver Rackham has called wildwood – primeval forest unaffected by the impact of human civilisation. Thanks to the work of Rackham and other researchers, we are beginning to have a picture of what the wildwood was like and how it developed after the arrival around 4000 BC of people who lived by farming. The wildwood was not a uniformly dense forest of noble trees, like the setting for a Robin Hood movie. It would have varied in composition and height according to local conditions, changes in climate and a variety of disasters of the sorts that through the ages have befallen natural forests everywhere.

There would have been clearings of various sizes as trees died or fell down; round their edges the new growth would have been kept down by grazing deer and wild cattle. Very much larger clearances would have been made by storms – the great storm that so surprised southern England on 16th October 1987, while very unusual, is by no means unique on the timescale of woodlands rather than of human lifespans; a storm of similar ferocity struck in 1703. The devastation may seem shocking, but it is not in reality a total disaster: in the short term, the sudden access of light to the woodland floor spurs a great burst of new growth, and the effect is enriching; in the longer term, woodlands, left to themselves, will regenerate naturally. The one form of catastrophe that the wildwood mainly escaped was fire – among our native trees, only the resinous Scots pine is at all flammable; the others, as Rackham puts it, burn like wet asbestos. It is a very different story, of course, for the plantations of alien conifers that attract the commercial foresters.

From about 4000 BC, when Britain's human population began to be farmers rather than hunter-gatherers, the demands of agriculture started to whittle away at the wildwood, partly through grazing and partly through clearance. The process gathered momentum from the beginning of the Bronze Age, around 2500 BC, and was at its peak in the early Iron Age, after 750 BC, when axes and ploughshares became commonplace. Oliver Rackham has estimated that by 500 BC half of England had ceased to be wildwood. When you think how much effort is involved, even with modern tools, in removing a single tree, the amount of labour that went into clearing such a vast area, albeit over some thousands of years, is almost unbelievable. But then, given the old picture of Britain as being completely primitive before the arrival of the Romans, so is the level of organisation behind the building of Stonehenge or the stone circles at Avebury, and they are still there as proof.

Long before humans started clearing woodland away in order to farm the land, they were already making use of it. The oldest wooden artefact found in Britain, the Clacton Bowstave, dates back to 40,000 years ago. It is made of yew, an astute choice, because yew is the hardest of all coniferous woods. The first wooden trackways across the peaty ground of the Somerset Levels date from about 3900 BC, and both the sizes and woods of the poles that were used were carefully matched to their particular purposes. The largest wooden structure ever built in Britain, the Bronze Age crannog at Flag Fen in Cambridgeshire, is an artificial island that covered four acres and supported many buildings. By the Iron Age, carpentry and wheel-wrighting had reached heights of sophistication that were not to be equalled for more than two thousand years.

When the Romans invaded in 55 and 54 BC, England already had a well-developed farming economy, and an important element in it was the management of woodlands. Our broad-leaved trees have one particular quality that is the key to traditional woodland management: if you cut them down, they spring up again, and, what is more, they

do so with amazing vigour, often growing to several feet in a single season. This makes them even more difficult to get rid of; the combination of felling and fire – called slash and burn – that can put paid for ever to the trees of the tropical rainforest just does not work in Britain.

In the most important woodland trees – oak, beech, hazel, ash, hornbeam, lime, wych elm, maple and alder – a crop of new shoots springs straight from the cut stump. This is the basis of coppicing, when the tree is cut close to the ground, and of pollarding, when at least six feet of trunk are left. In a few trees – sallow, aspen, cherry and English elm – the trunk dies, and the root system sends up new shoots (suckers) around the dead stump. This is how elms that have been killed by Dutch elm disease come to be surrounded by thickets of healthy saplings.

Coppicing goes back a long way before the beginning of recorded history – the earliest of the trackways across the Somerset Levels, constructed around 3900 BC, appears to have been made of wood from coppiced trees. Before there were metal tools to split wood, it

was poles from coppice that were useful rather than large timber from mature tree trunks. This was the case for a very long time: as long, indeed, as it was easier to select a pole of the right size than to machine down something larger.

Even by today's standards, Roman Britain was not very heavily wooded. In Roman England, no more than a quarter of the wildwood remained, and most of that was very far from being undisturbed. The pattern of the countryside as we know it today, including hedges, had probably begun to appear before the Romans arrived. It used to be thought that the villages mentioned in the Domesday Book had grown up in the centuries immediately before its compilation in 1086, but it now seems more likely that many of the settlements and other features of the countryside go back much further. Apart from the timber they needed for building, the Romans also used large quantities of wood to fuel their industrial developments. They would have had to exploit the remarkable productivity of coppice as well as its cut-and-come-again quality. Oliver Rackham has calculated that the wood from 23,000 acres of coppice was needed to sustain the output of the Roman military ironworks in the Weald.

The departure of the Romans from 410 onwards was followed by a massive drop in population, possibly because of the plague. The Roman towns fell into disrepair, and in some parts of the countryside woodland reappeared where agricultural land had been abandoned. But this process cannot have been very extensive, as the Domesday Book reveals that only half the settlements that it recorded in any detail had woodland; great areas had virtually none.

Thanks to the Robin Hood legend, what is most remembered about the Norman kings is their addiction to hunting, which led to draconian laws to protect the Royal Forests and the deer they contained. How far these laws were enforced is another matter, but the Royal Forests also had other functions. It did not take the third of the kingdom that they covered to cater for the recreational needs of the court. Apart from providing the king with large quantities of venison (most of it killed by professional huntsmen), the Royal Forests also yielded revenue from their produce and from a variety of rents, taxes and fines and, through Forest Law, they increased the king's control over a large part of his realm. Much of the area covered by the Royal Forests was not actually wooded; within their bounds were whole counties such as Essex and Huntingdon.

The medieval idea of a forest, whether or not it was owned by the king, was very different from ours: it was defined in terms of hunting rather than of trees and contained everything from thick woodland to pasture, arable land and settlements. The inhabitants of the towns and villages often depended for their survival on their common rights of grazing and collecting wood, which were limited by Forest Law only where they conflicted with hunting. In contrast to the way it is seen and treated today, woodland in medieval times (and for that matter at any time from prehistory up to perhaps two hundred years ago) was regarded as an asset and managed to make it as productive as possible. Its main justification was not as a haven for wildlife, an amenity providing spiritual refreshment for townspeople or a decorative part of the landscape; it was a key part of the economy of the countryside. The aesthetic pleasure that we now derive from woodlands is not just a gift from nature but the result of the way they were managed in the past.

In the organisation of rural life, everything had its place, which was determined by experience rather than by theory. The places in a parish with the least fertile soil were the most likely to be left as woodland, which was then managed to produce as much as possible of what was most needed. This was not, in the main, great timbers but smaller wood.

The three main uses for wood were for building, for fencing and as fuel. The traditional English method of building is wattle and daub, which goes back at least to Anglo-Saxon times. It combines small branches with a mixture of clay, lime and water, which has sometimes been supplemented with dung or straw, to produce a remarkably sturdy and long-lasting material. The frame of the building, even if it was quite grand, still did not involve any very large timber; for most buildings, the wood could be obtained from coppice. Oliver Rackham records that the 1400 oaks that went into the Old Court of Corpus Christi College, Cambridge, were mainly under nine inches in diameter. It was economical in every sense never to use wood that was larger than was absolutely necessary – the rounded corners of the timbers in old houses are actually the outside of the log.

Thin coppice wood was woven into wattle fencing. The smallest wood of all – brushwood – was bundled up as faggots to use as fuel. Nothing was wasted. For most rural purposes, it did not matter much what sort of tree provided the wood, and coppices, at least until the seventeenth century, were a mixture of whatever happened to be growing there. Actually planting enough trees to make up a wood did not come into fashion until well after 1600, and for a long time it was mainly coppice that was planted.

Up to about 1750, the two typical sorts of English woodland were wood-pasture and coppice. Commons were very often wood-pasture, on which the commoners had the right to gather firewood and graze their animals. Grazing had to be carefully regulated so that it did not stop the trees regenerating. The trees on commons were very often pollards, which made them less vulnerable: the great pollarded beeches of Frithsden in Hertfordshire were originally surrounded by wood-pasture.

Coppice also helped feed animals, and people as well. The delicious nuts produced by hazel coppice were worth gathering for human consumption, and there was a tradition of pannage – letting pigs out into the woods in autumn to gorge themselves on acorns or sometimes beechmast – which could produce extra revenue for the holder of the land. The commonest form of coppice included larger trees (called standards), notably oaks, which were not cut down with the rest of the coppice but allowed to grow and eventually felled as large timber. This was a splendidly efficient system because the coppice could provide for those who relied on the wood while the standards built up as a capital asset.

Coppice is an extremely good environment for wild animals and plants. As coppicing was organised on the principle of rotation, with a portion cut down each year, woodlands contained coppice at all stages of growth. Animals and plants could thus thrive in the sort of coppice that suited them best. The animals could move from one part of a wood to another, and plants could survive through each cycle of coppicing to burgeon when the conditions were right, usually just after cutting. As the shade deepened, they either hung on in a not very vigorous way or stayed as seeds in the soil, often for many years – incredibly, the wood spurge is known to have grown from seed after 120 years. When the coppice was cut, the plants would spring up again in a riot of growth and flowering.

Some trees did have special uses from very early times, even though they were not grown for the purpose. The inner bark of lime trees, called bast, was used as a fibre, notably in rope-making; its soft, even-grained wood was beloved of woodcarvers and allowed Grinling

17

Gibbons to produce carvings of astonishing virtuosity. Hornbeam was so hard that it could be used for cogs and pulleys. Ash wood was tough but elastic and so made good wheel spokes and wagon frames as well as the walking sticks for which it has most recently been known. Oak, of course, was the great wood of the builder and the shipwright (whose need for curved timbers to shape into ships' hulls was better provided for by trees from hedgerows and park land than by woodland oaks).

Over the past thousand years, the fortunes of woodland have inevitably varied considerably according to the activities of the human population. In the years after the Domesday Book in 1086, the population grew very fast, at least doubling in the next 160 years, and the pressure on the land meant that woodland was destroyed at the rate of twenty acres a day. The destruction was finally halted by the Black Death in 1349, and it was not until the sixteenth or seventeenth century that the population caught up with the land that was available to feed it.

From Tudor times, the situation became more complicated. The demand for timber was increased by such factors as building in towns, the change from home fires smouldering in the middle of the floor to burning in a chimney and even the expansion of hop-growing, which needed lots of large poles. Set against this was the introduction of coal, which was already the main fuel in the cities by the beginning of the seventeenth century.

Wood was also a crucial raw material for industry. Iron smelting and other industries that used charcoal were situated in wooded areas, as they had been since before the arrival of the Romans. Until recently, the ironworks were blamed for destroying woodland, but in fact they could obtain the vast quantities of wood they needed only through the productiveness of coppice. If anything, the industries which had an insatiable appetite for wood actually helped to preserve woodland.

It was not until after 1750 that things began definitively to change. Coke was increasingly replacing charcoal for industry, which moved out of the woodlands and into the coalfields. The price of timber started to go up sharply in relation to that of smaller wood from coppice, partly because of the boom in shipbuilding – it is said that more timber-built shipping was launched between 1800 and 1860 than in the whole of British history before then.

While coppice shrank as its markets disappeared, the demand for timber led to new woodland being planted to produce it. The wonderful beech woods of the Chilterns did not get there because of any particular affinity of beech trees for the flinty soil of the area or for the underlying chalk but because they were planted to produce raw material for the furniture industry centred in High Wycombe. Oaks had a double appeal: their biggest market from 1780 to 1850 was not the Navy and probably not the merchant fleet but the booming leather industry, which used oak bark in tanning. It was this as much as anything that encouraged large-scale planting of oaks in the first half of the nineteenth century.

The serious decline of coppice began with the railways, which made coal available cheaply in the countryside as well as in the cities. This removed coppice wood's last important use, as fuel, leaving only hurdle-making and other woodland industries, which were all but wiped out by the agricultural depression of the 1930s.

The Victorian era brought another development that has had disastrous consequences. German foresters, who had worked for the British colonial authorities in India and Cyprus, came back to this country, bringing with them the German idea of forestry, which saw trees in straightforward economic terms as a crop to be planted and harvested. What they believed in were conifers, which had been grown in German plantations since 1368 and seemed to offer the best (that is to say, quickest) cash return.

Forestry in the German manner had empire-building tendencies that were quite alien to the British tradition of woodmanship. Conifer forests began to be planted, not just on moors and second-rate farmland but on ancient woodlands, which were just in the way.

One of the most influential of the foresters was William Schlich, who became Professor of Forestry at Oxford in 1906. He was also a member of the committee that recommended the setting up of the Forestry Commission in 1919. The Commission started out to blanket the countryside with mainly coniferous plantations that were justified on grounds of national security as well as economics: no longer would U-boat blockades be able to run us short of timber. It took some time for a bad idea to grow into a national disaster: although there were some exceptions, notably in South Wales and on sites for airfields, virtually all the ancient woods that existed when the Forestry Commission was founded were still there in 1950.

Anyone with an interest in the countryside must be only too painfully aware of what has happened since then. In the thirty years after World War II, nearly half the ancient woodland in Britain was destroyed – as much as in the previous four hundred years. The trees were killed by ring-barking or poisoning and the stumps were dragged out by bulldozers to make way for conifers and arable prairies.

The climate has now changed. Thanks to a lot of mainly unwelcome developments in agriculture, there is now too much farming land rather than too little. The economic justifications for afforestation have fallen apart under scrutiny. Public hostility to the foresters was heightened in the 'eighties as the news leaked out that government support for forestry had given it the new function of providing tax breaks for show business personalities and peers of the realm at the expense of smothering yet more of our natural heritage under Christmas trees.

The future of our ancient woodlands is still very much in the balance, but at least there is a widespread sense of their value. One approach might be to direct efforts into finding important uses for the wood that British coppice can produce so efficiently. This is at odds with the present industrial view of wood. 'Our age,' writes Rackham, 'treats timber as if it were plastic. Sawmills and other machines are designed to reduce trees, regardless of their natural shapes, to exact rectangular sections.'

Most attempts to destroy more of our woodland are now met with determined opposition, very often with success, as in the case of Oxleas Wood in Greenwich. There are still myths to be combatted, like the idea that aged trees are geriatric trees and likely to be dangerous. There will still be wrong turnings, like the sometimes ill-advised initiatives for replanting damaged woodland rather than simply letting it regenerate.

But at least the will is there among the general public, and there is a chance that they may drag the politicians along with them. What we must never forget is that the reasons for saving our woodlands cannot be reduced to practical considerations of economic use or wildlife conservation. They have a spiritual dimension that touches all of us. Nothing can replace the incalculable value of dappled sunlight and birdsong, of briefly glimpsed woodland creatures and of mossy banks strewn with primroses and violets. It is a part of our heritage that we cannot afford to be without.

The flowers of the blackthorn, which very much later in the year will turn into sloes, appear on its bare, blackish twigs well before any trees or shrubs are in leaf. As early as March, they lighten the edges of woodlands with a soft fuzz of creamy white.

Hazel is another shrub which has flowers that appear before the leaves, sometimes as early as January. The long, tasselly catkins are made up of the male flowers; the little tufts of female flowers, less than a quarter of an inch long, are much less conspicuous. Left to itself, the hazel can become a small tree, but traditionally it has been coppiced and cut regularly. Nowadays, most hazel coppices that have not been grubbed up are neglected and overgrown.

Scatters of delicate white wood anemone flowers are among the most delightful sights of early spring. They are a sure sign that woodland is ancient – the wood anemone is such a poor coloniser that even after hundreds of years it may have failed to establish itself in apparently suitable places.

Even in winter, the wild cherry is easy to recognise because of its smooth reddish-brown bark, which peels off in thin strips. Its flowers make delicate patches of white on the edges of woods at the time when the trees are coming into leaf and everything is beginning to look fresh and green.

It is the male cuckoo, like the one in my picture, whose call carries so well and gives the bird its name. The female makes a long chuckling sound. The call of the cuckoo, a bird that is in general heard and not seen, is the sound that above all others makes me feel that spring has come to the woodlands, and I never fail to be thrilled the first time I hear it each year. It is not surprising that this sound has been so celebrated in poetry and music, not to mention letters to *The Times*. I have been happy to find that there seem to be more cuckoos around in 1993, at least in my area of Hertfordshire, than I have heard for some time: as many as five in a square mile.

Bluebell woods are one of the wonders of the world, and nowhere are they more spectacular than in Britain. The carpets of violet-blue flowers shimmering under the dappled spring sunlight in a hazel coppice or oak wood are an unforgettable sight. For this book, I have painted bluebell woods in Buckinghamshire and, with fallow deer which leave the poisonous bluebell plants alone, in Dorset.

27

The damp climate of Britain clearly suits bluebells, and in Cornwall they even thrive away from woodlands, turning the cliff tops blue. Over most of southern England, however, they seem to need the moist atmosphere of woodlands, though they will survive in hedges and under bracken where the trees that have sheltered them from time immemorial have been destroyed.

Bluebells spread very slowly – the heavy black seeds that drop out of their seedcases are unlikely to travel very far – and bluebell woods are mostly ancient in origin. This means that even if modern tree plantations were suitable for bluebells (which they are not), it would take a very long time – centuries perhaps – for new woodland to develop the swathes of flowers that are a springtime national treasure. Our ancient bluebell woods are irreplaceable, and, like woods in general, have fallen victim to the government-encouraged greed of farmers and foresters.

In a wood filled with ramsons (wild garlic) the smell may be very far from the magical scent of bluebells, but the starry white flowers look very attractive covering the woodland floor.

This scene of a bridle path and woodland is a moonlit May night on the Gaddesden estate in Hertfordshire. The time of year is the same in my picture of badgers, although there it is earlier in the evening – that stage of dusk when everything stops: the wind has dropped and no birds are singing.

If you have been waiting very quietly, it is at this point that you are likely to catch your first glimpse of stripey heads. I have shown the badgers when they have just emerged from the sett and are waving their heads from side to side to pick up scents. With their poor eyesight, they rely heavily on their sense of smell to tell them of danger or to help them forage for their food, which can include anything from small rodents to slugs, even whole nests of wasps. Badgers are now protected by law against all the terrible things that were done to them in the past. Their main enemy is now motor transport. In my view, the badgers were here first and should be given total protection with whatever fencing and other precautions are necessary.

Greater stitchwort forms mats of bluish green foliage dotted with white flowers along hedgerows and the edges of woods, particularly ancient ones. Wild arum or lords-and-ladies is an aggressive coloniser and can survive in quite deep shade. My painting puts together the flowers and the fruit, which appear a few months apart.

The rosebay willowherb is as much of an opportunist among plants as the fox is among mammals. In the nineteenth century, it was restricted to rocky places. Particularly since the war, it has spread at a phenomenal rate, taking advantage of the destruction of woodlands and colonising disturbed ground everywhere. It brought great splashes of purplish pink to London's bomb sites – its other, very appropriate name is fireweed.

The little owl hunts by day as well as at dusk and has prospered in England since its introduction from continental Europe at the end of the nineteenth century. Here it is wearing its characteristic expression: fierce yellow eyes set in a perpetual frown.

The spectacular thing about the nightingale is its song; you very rarely see the bird itself, which is only a little larger than a robin. Because it nests close to the ground, the nightingale prefers coppice at its densest stage, and the decline in coppicing has inevitably led to a decline in the nightingale population. It sings not from the tops of trees but from bushes or even while on the ground and is as vocal during the day as it is at night, but it comes into its own in the evenings when most other woodland birds have fallen silent.

The brimstone and the comma are both butterflies that can be found on the edges of woodland. Both emerge from hibernation and lay their eggs in the spring – the brimstone, which is particularly fond of ivy-covered trees, is the earliest of our butterflies to appear – and both are at their most plentiful in July and August.

The white admiral is one of the most striking butterflies of mature woodlands, where it can be seen gliding gracefully across rides. It is very likely to settle on brambles, the flowers of which it seems to find particularly attractive.

I have always loved the delicacy of white butterflies on dandelion clocks or thistledown. This picture shows two species that are found in woodland clearings. At the top is the wood white, the smallest and most fragile-looking of our white butterflies, which has a somewhat mechanical-seeming flight. Slightly larger and more common is the green-veined white, which likes rather sunnier places.

Red admirals stay on the wing all through the autumn, which is why I like to paint them on blackberries or other fruit. They rarely survive hibernation, and migrants from the continent arrive each May to lay the eggs that will develop into our main summer and autumn population.

The lapwings in my picture are flying through the sort of landscape that we need to preserve. Saving woodlands is fine, but they must not be left isolated in a sea of intensive desolation, so that anything that emerges has to run the gauntlet of chemical-laden prairies. I like to see woods connected by a network of hedges, which can work as an extension of the woodland and amount to a sort of road system for wildlife. And, of course, a hedge of any age that has not been sprayed and flailed into submission will have a rich fauna of its own.

The detail of hops, haws and blackberries shows a section of a very large hedge in Cambridgeshire at a stage when it was laden with fruit. I could have taken any other portion of it and had as lavish a selection, all providing wildlife with a rich source of food for the autumn and winter. This is exactly what is removed if the hedges are constantly cut back to keep them tidy.

The wren and the goldcrest are the two smallest breeding birds in Britain. The wren spends its time busily searching for food in tangled undergrowth and dense bushes, never flying further than is necessary to get to the next feeding place. Because it almost always stays in thick cover, it is easy to forget that the wren is one of our commonest birds. The goldcrest is even smaller and flits in a quiet, rather discreet way from twig to twig or tree to tree. It is not as shy as you might expect; if you stay still in the right place, goldcrests will come quite close. I have painted them here in autumn with spindle fruit and sloes.

This is a clearing in an oakwood which I have painted to express my enjoyment of the colours and textures of early autumn. It would have been easy to add a foreground subject, but here I wanted to concentrate on the beauty of the wood itself, the tranquillity of the clearing with the track going off invitingly into the distance, and the colours of the oak leaves just beginning to turn.

The oak, commemorated in innumerable pub signs, has an almost mystical association with England: an oak tree, still standing today, sheltered Charles II from his pursuers after the battle of Worcester in 1651, and the ships that over three centuries established Britain's naval power were built of oak. From the toughness of its wood came

that old metaphor for bravery: heart of oak. But the toughness came from slow growth, and in an era when it is only too easy to import hardwood torn out of the rain forests, the oak is a poor proposition for commercial forestry.

The pattern of fallen oak leaves lying on the woodland floor always reminds me of a jigsaw puzzle: they look to me as if they somehow ought to interlock.

I have always liked to paint game birds such as woodcock and pheasant against the autumnal tones of dead bracken and fallen leaves that pick up the colours in their plumage, and the monochrome effect produces an overall impression of mellowness.

In fact, you would be more likely to see woodcock in the spring, at mating time, when the males perform their noisy display flights, called roding, at dawn and dusk. Mainly, during the day, they lurk motionless in cover like the woodcock in my painting, merging with the landscape. The only way that you are likely to see one during the day is if you happen to flush it from the undergrowth, when it will take off very fast, zigzagging through the trees.

As late as 1920, a bird book could describe the woodcock as '*the bird of the sportsman*'. Before guns came into use, the woodcock was caught by 'cock-shooting' – nets were placed across angles cut into the outlines of woods to catch the birds as they returned from nocturnal expeditions to the marshes and ditches where they found their food. There were even specially shaped cock-shoot woods that were designed with this in mind.

In the woodlands of two hundred years ago, woodcock were still more plentiful than pheasants, and coppicing provided ideal cover for them. Since then, nothing has happened to favour the survival of the woodcock, while the pheasant, which will obligingly lay as many as fifteen eggs in a brood and lends itself to being reared in captivity to keep up the number of targets, has become big business.

For me, the sound of a cock pheasant's call echoing through the damp autumn woods is the essence of that time of year, just as the song of the cuckoo and the sight of orange tip butterflies are hallmarks of spring.

Although the pheasant is not a native of this country, it has been here for a long time, and the provisions that have been made for it have meant that it has perhaps had a greater influence on the English landscape than any other bird. The first known mention of it is in a document from the court of King Harold in 1059. Thomas à Becket, Archbishop of Canterbury, is said to have enjoyed a dinner of pheasant on the night before his murder by Henry II's knights in 1170.

The bird remained fairly scarce until the early nineteenth century when Lord Leicester at Holkham Hall in Norfolk developed the 'modern' system of pheasant shooting, with platoons of beaters and the slaughter on a grand scale of pheasants on the wing. Neglected woodlands were improved or replanted, and new tree plantations were grown specifically as pheasant coverts. By the 1860s, when the Prince of Wales bought Sandringham to develop for the purpose, pheasant shooting was already firmly established as the pastime of grandees; its popularity has since become ever more general.

Under the old trees in this very open beech wood, there is hardly any undergrowth – the dense foliage does not let through enough light for much to grow. What there is, though, is something else that is important in the life of the woodlands: the dead timber rotting on the ground which is the home of a rich population of woodlice, insects and, of course, fungi.

My study of fungi shows five types that are quite common in our woodlands. I am particularly attracted by their sculptural qualities, which make them delightful subjects. I have painted four edible types and one that very definitely is not: the orangey-red fly agaric, which may belong with elves and fairies in the woodland mythology of Victorian illustrators, but is poisonous, if not quite as deadly as some of its less striking relatives. The others are the bare-edged russula at the top left, a parasol mushroom below it, the oyster mushroom on the right and the common puff-ball at the bottom.

54

This Buckinghamshire landscape is a piece of everyday countryside crossed by hedgerows, with a small wood on the horizon that might well have been planted in the last century to provide cover for game. Just because it seems not to be very special, it is easy to forget that it is important, but in fact it is the very fabric of the countryside. Saving what is rare or unusual is to be applauded, but the fate of the countryside as a whole should be of equal concern to us.

A countryside of woods and hedgerows is the ideal home for small parties of long-tailed tits as they flit about constantly making their thin little calls. I have painted them in winter when they are easier to see among the bare branches. In cold weather, they look like tiny balls of feathers with a diminutive beak at one end and a very long tail at the other.

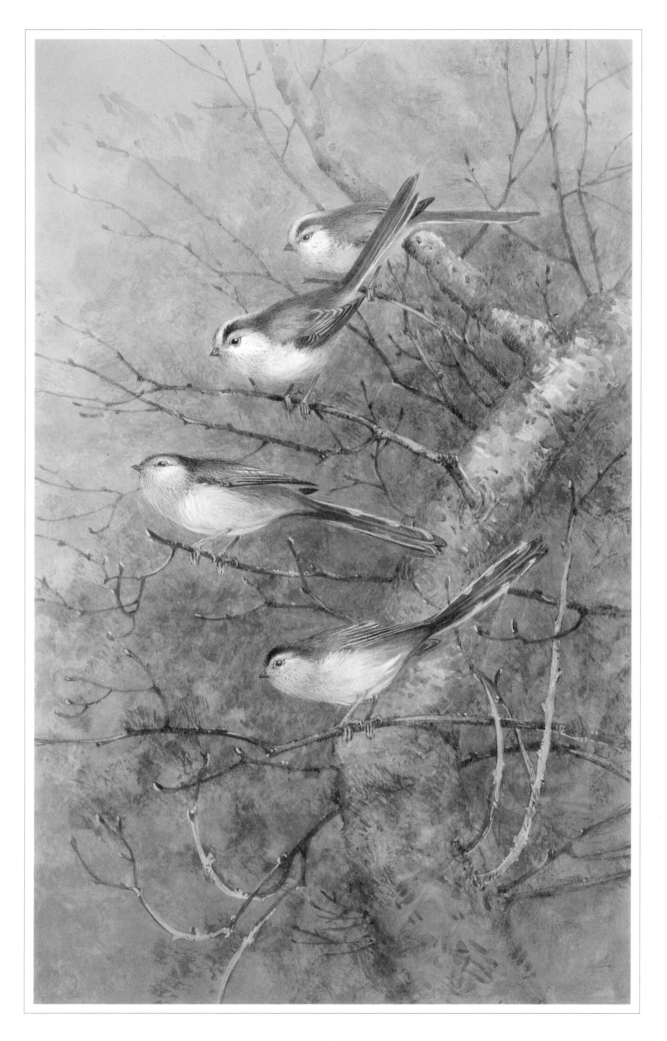

Woodland trees have a rich fauna of insects, and these in turn help support some of our most attractive birds. The treecreeper can usually be glimpsed working its way up a tree trunk with jerky mouse-like movements, picking insects and spiders out from the bark. The great spotted woodpecker uses the amazing force of its bill to extract wood-boring insects and to make its unmistakable staccato drumming sound on rotten branches.

The nuthatch is another insect-eater, but it is equally keen on seeds and nuts, which it wedges into crevices and breaks open, putting all the strength of its short, rather cigar-shaped body behind the blows from its beak. I have drawn it in a very characteristic pose as it moves restlessly down a rotten branch.

Where nuthatches are reasonably common in the woodlands of Englands and Wales, the red squirrel has all but vanished, for reasons that are not entirely clear. I have most recently seen them in Belgium. Their place has been taken by the grey squirrel, an altogether more destructive animal, which was introduced from North America a century or so ago and has become a considerable pest.

The drawings of fallow deer are taken from sketches that I have made over the last few years. Unlike the red and roe deer, the fallow deer is not an indigenous British species, but in comparison with the muntjac and sika deer that are also found wild in Britain, it has been around so long that it seems very much to belong here.

Originally from Asia, it is known to have been kept by the Romans. Whether or not they brought it to Britain with them, it was certainly imported by the Normans around 1100 to keep in parks. Maintaining deer parks has always been a costly business as it takes a very big barrier to confine an animal as strong and agile as a deer. Even so, Oliver Rackham has estimated that by 1300 there were as many as 3,200 parks in England. They took in about a quarter of the country's woodlands and provided the rich and powerful with venison for their tables – salt venison was greatly favoured by medieval kings – and sometimes with the sport of hunting.

Although fallow deer have traditionally been kept in wooded parks, they can cause considerable damage to woodlands by stripping bark in winter and by eating young shoots. After coppice has been cut, it has to be fenced until the new growth is tall enough to be out of reach to deer; one of the advantages of pollarding, in which the branches were cut off several feet from the ground, was that the new growth was high enough up to be safe.

Even today, there are still great parks like that of Woburn Abbey in Bedfordshire and Richmond Park in Surrey which maintain herds of fallow deer. Over the centuries, animals have inevitably escaped and their descendants are found in the wild in suitable forest areas all over England. There are many of them at Ashridge, near my home in Hertfordshire.

In the picture of the white fallow buck on the next page, I have cleared away the foreground foliage that would normally obscure the animals. I prefer to watch fallow deer in genuinely wild surroundings

like the dense, swampy woodland of Powerstock in Dorset, where you can hear the buzzards mewing above the tops of the trees. It was here that a friend and I, after several hours of working our way slowly into the depths of the forest, had the unforgettable experience of observing the deer rutting: the musky smell of the animals, the roaring of the displaying bucks, the hinds squealing and the noise of them all crashing about in the vegetation.

When they are not grazing, fallow deer normally stay in cover, like those I have painted in the shade of two beeches. Many of the great, pollarded trees like these, which gave their name to Frithsden Beeches in Hertfordshire, have now gone. Once, they were pollarded regularly as a sustainable source of timber, but they have not been managed in this way for at least a century, and some, like those in my picture, now have boughs that sag right down to the ground, as if they were trying to prop up the tree – and well they might, for in recent years many of them have been toppled by gales.

Everyone thinks of the hare – I am talking here about the brown or common hare as opposed to the Scottish or mountain hare which is a creature of moors and uplands – as an animal of open fields. However, it depends very much on woodlands and hedgerows for shelter, coming out into the fields to feed at night. Where rabbits make burrows to retreat to, hares scrape out shallow indentations called forms, which are used repeatedly unless they are disturbed. These are usually in long grass or under the cover of shrubs such as brambles, but are occasionally out in the open.

Normally, in daytime, a hare will nestle down in the form with its long ears laid back along its head, sometimes with only its back and head

visible. If it senses danger, its reaction is to flatten itself even further, and only when the threat gets very close will it make a dash for it – with its proverbial speed, the hare can outrun most predators.

The perfect grazing place for a hare is a traditional hay meadow which is subjected only to an annual mowing and has a great richness of plants which provide the varied diet that it needs. In this country, the hare population has declined seriously because almost every feature of recent farming practice has worked against it: sheltering hedgerows and woodlands have been ripped out and grassland is sprayed with toxic herbicides to remove any unscheduled plant life and leave only vast areas of sterile monoculture that can be cut twice a year. It has not been helped either by stubble burning (which puts a stop to any tender new growth that could provide autumn food) or by the booming population of foxes, which prey on it. The hare I have shown on the next page in an open landscape has left some woodland and crossed a stubble field, making for more cover.

The dormouse is another mammal that is in decline, and the key reason, as usual, is habitat destruction. Its ideal home is hazel coppice that is cut regularly but not too freqently, so that it grows large enough to produce crops of nuts; neglected and overgrown coppice shades out the bush layer that provides the dormouse with its food.

In the places where it lives, the dormouse is not very much in evidence. It hibernates for about half the year and sleeps during the day, emerging only at night. Even then, it does not move very far. One sign of its presence is hazel nuts that show the dormouse's own particular style of neatly gnawed hole. The Mammal Society believes that there are dormice in the Gade Valley, where I live, but I have not seen one here. Mr Fowler, who grew up in my house the best part of a century ago, had a pet dormouse, which he fed with bits of biscuit when it came out in the evening. He never knew where it lived, but when the house was recently modernised, we found a great heap of empty walnut shells inside the staircase.

The fox is the great survivor among our mammals. The secret of its amazing success is adaptability. Its diet has always included carrion as well as live animals and birds; the modern urban or suburban fox has developed this side of its country cousins' diet by diversifying into dustbin clearance. I have been observing and drawing foxes for many years and making studies, trying to catch them in characteristic poses, as in the sketch at the bottom of the opposite page which shows one stalking, just before it makes that final leap in the air to seize its prey.

The inspiration for the painting on this page came on a bitterly cold winter day. I was standing in a wood when a fox appeared through a gap in the vegetation. He stopped by a tree and looked around – which is how I have caught him here. Then he grew concerned, probably because he had become aware of my presence, and went off, but not in any great hurry.

The willow tit (above) and the redpoll (opposite) are both birds that are found on the edges of woods and in damp birch or alder woods. I have painted the redpolls as I can see them in winter just outside my gate on the dead reeds and great hairy willowherb along the wooded banks of the river Gade.

The tree I have sketched is a maple in parkland with a wood behind containing a rookery, a typical detail of Hertfordshire landscape.

The final picture in this book is of one of my favourite woodland birds, the tawny owl, in the sort of setting in which you might see it during the day. If you look up under a big, thick stand of holly in a mixed woodland, you may well see a tawny owl roosting in the gloom.